WONDER STARTERS

Hair

Pictures by CHRISTINE SHARR

Published by WONDER BOOKS
A Division of Grosset & Dunlap, Inc.
A NATIONAL GENERAL COMPANY
51 Madison Avenue   New York, N.Y. 10010

About Wonder Starters

Wonder Starters are vocabulary controlled information books for young children. More than ninety per cent of the words in the text will be in the reading vocabulary of the vast majority of young readers. Word and sentence length have also been carefully controlled.

Key new words associated with the topic of each book are repeated with picture explanations in the Starters dictionary at the end. The dictionary can also be used as an index for teaching children to look things up.

Teachers and experts have been consulted on the content and accuracy of the books.

Published in the United States by Wonder Books, a Division of Grosset & Dunlap, Inc., a National General Company.

ISBN: 0-448-09650-1 (Trade Edition)
ISBN: 0-448-06370-0 (Library Edition)

FIRST PRINTING 1972

Printed and bound in the United States.

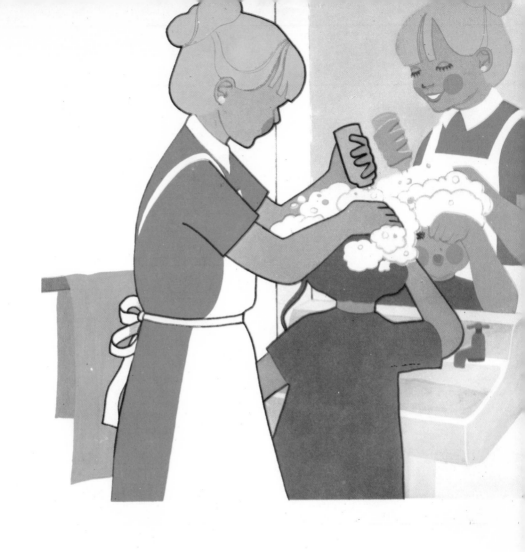

Mommy is washing my hair.
I have shampoo in my eyes.

I am rubbing my hair
with a towel.
Soon it will be dry.
2

Now I must brush my hair.
I make a part
with a comb.

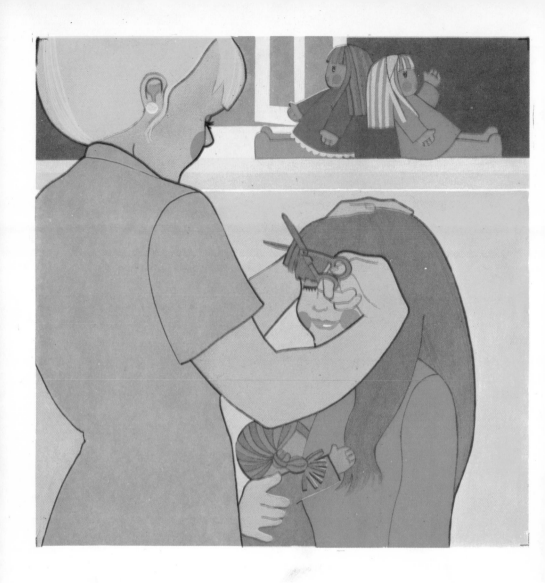

My hair is very long.
My bangs are long.
So Mommy cuts my hair.
4

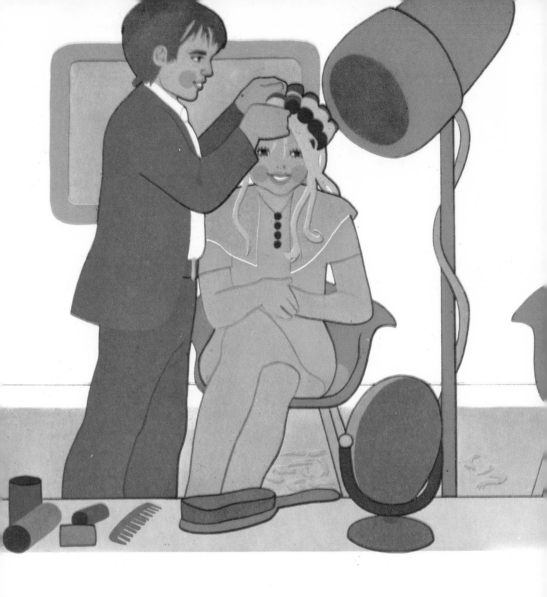

Mommy is at the hairdresser.
The hairdresser has cut her hair.
Now he is making her hair curly.

Some people's hair is always curly.
Some people have straight hair.
6

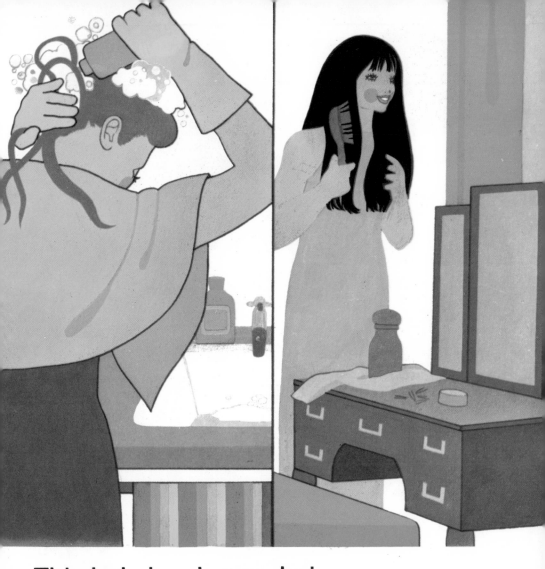

This lady has brown hair.
She does not want brown hair.
So she dyes her hair.
She dyes her hair black.

7

Some ladies wear wigs.

Sometimes men wear wigs.
This man has a gray wig.
He is a judge.
He lives in England.

Long ago
lots of men wore wigs.
Their wigs were very long.
10

The ladies wore wigs, too.
Sometimes they wore huge wigs.

11

This man lived in China.
He had long hair.
He wore his hair in a braid.
12

Some men still have long hair.
Pop singers often have long hair.

Men have hair
on their chins.
Sometimes they let it grow
into a beard.
14

This man is a monk.
He has cut off all his hair.

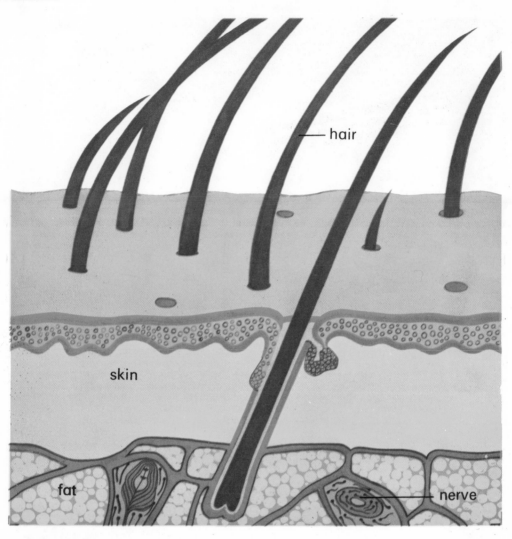

People have thousands of hairs
on their heads.
Each hair grows
out of a tiny hole.

Hairs often fall out.
These are old hairs.
New hairs usually take their place.

17

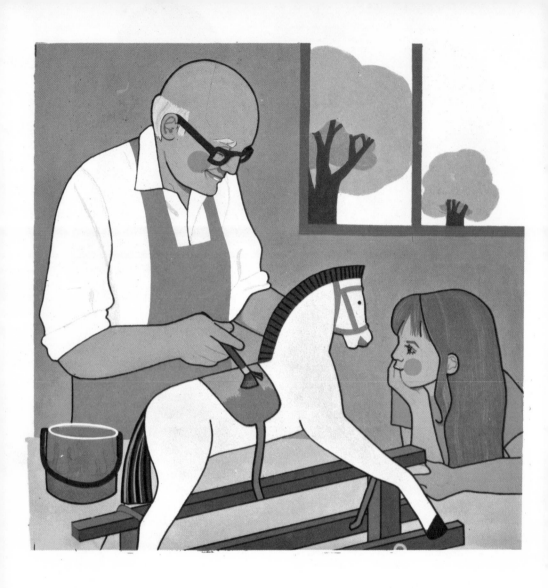

When no new hair grows,
people go bald.
Grandfather is bald.
18

Some old people have white hair.
Grandmother has white hair.

Some animals have hair
all over them.
Dogs have hair.
Horses and zebras have hair.
20

This animal is a rhinoceros.
Its horn is like lots of hairs.
They grow together
to make a hard horn.

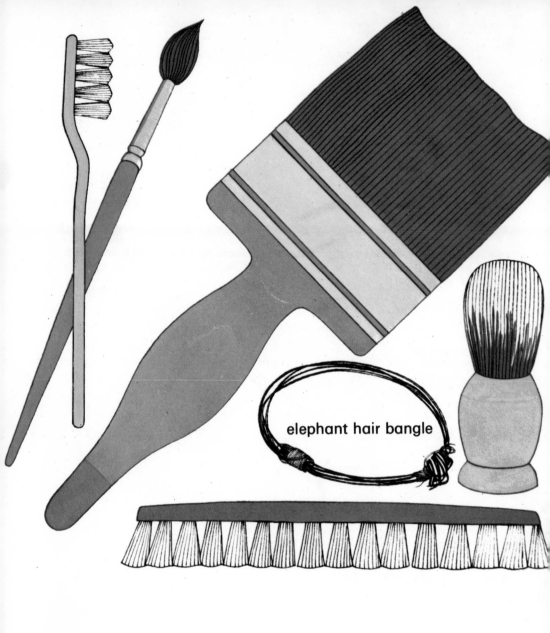

elephant hair bangle

All these things are made of hair.

22

Starter's **Hair** words

wash
(page 1)

brush
(page 3)

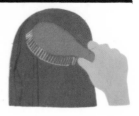

shampoo
(page 1)

part
(page 3)

rub
(page 2)

comb
(page 3)

towel
(page 2)

long hair
(page 4)

bangs
(page 4)

dye
(page 7)

cut
(page 4)

wig
(page 8)

hairdresser
(page 5)

judge
(page 9)

curly
(page 5)

England
(page 9)

straight
(page 6)

China
(page 12)

24

braid
(page 12)

pop singer
(page 13)

beard
(page 14)

monk
(page 15)

bald
(page 18)

dog
(page 20)

horse
(page 20)

zebra
(page 20)

rhinoceros
(page 21)

horn
(page 21)